Y0-BVQ-839

GEMINI HOROSCOPE
2015

Lisa Lazuli

Lisa Lazuli is the author of the amazon bestseller

HOROSCOPE 2014: ASTROLOGY and NUMEROLOGY HOROSCOPES

ABOUT THE AUTHOR

Lisa Lazuli studied astrology with the Faculty of Astrological Studies in London.

She has practiced since 1999.

Lisa has been a regular guest on BBWM and BBC Shropshire talking about astrology and doing both horoscopes and live readings. She has also made guest appearances on Fox FM, BBC Cambridgeshire, BBC Northamptonshire, BBC Coventry and Warwickshire and US Internet Radio Shows including the Debra Clement Show.

Lisa wrote horoscopes for Asian Woman Magazine.

Now available:

TAURUS: Your Day, Your Decan, Your Sign

Includes 2015 Predictions.

The most REVEALING book on The Bull yet.

And

ARIES HOROSCOPE 2015

TAURUS HOROSCOPE 2015

Lisa Lazuli is also the author of

The mystery/thrillers:

A Sealed Fate

Holly Leaves

Next of Sin

<u>As well as:</u>

Delicious, Nutritious Recipes for the Time and Cash Strapped

Paleo Diet: Get Started, Get Motivated, Feel Great.

99 ACE Places to Promote Your Book

Pressure Cooking Reinvented.

Be Wine Savvy

If you would like me to calculate your natal chart FREE of charge based on your time, date and place of birth click here:

http://lisalazuli.com/2014/06/30/would-you-like-to-know-where-all-your-planets-are-free-natal-chart/

Contents

Dear Reader,

I hope my yearly horoscope for Gemini will provide you with some insightful guidance during what is a very tricky time astrologically speaking with the heavy planets i.e. Pluto and Uranus at loggerheads in cardinal signs and Neptune in Pisces calling us all to get in touch with our spiritual side.

I have a conversational style of writing, please excuse any grammatical errors, I write much as I would speak.

As the song goes, "Nobody said it was easy." I know the mass media pump-out shows us plenty about quick fix love, money, fame and success; however, life is a journey filled with challenges and obstacles designed to encourage us to find out what we are made of and who we really are.

Embrace the good and bad and enjoy what is your unique experience.

Be the hero in your own personal life movie and never hide your spotlight.

I must add that the best astrology insights are gained from a unique chart based on your time, date, year and place of birth.

If you would like your natal chart calculated for FREE:

http://lisalazuli.com/2014/06/30/would-you-like-to-know-where-all-your-planets-are-free-natal-chart/:

Join me on facebook at:

https://www.facebook.com/pages/Lisa-Lazuli-Astrologer/192000594298158?ref=hl

A year of great willpower, where you can use your strength and courage to break down barriers and achieve your aims and ambitions. Filled with energy and motivation, you won't be hanging about, you will have the oomph to really crack on with tasks and make good progress. This is especially true in the second half of the year.

This is the year to take control of your health – you may take on a new diet or exercise regime, and you will stick to it. In the same vein, you will have a renewed confidence in dealing with people and will find that it is easier to stand up for yourself and get yourself noticed. Your approach to living is very forthright and upfront; this is not a year when you will take a long time to make decisions, you are spontaneous and will go for things. There is a spirit of both adventure and self-improvement – you want to try new things not just for the sake of excitement, but for the possibilities it offers you to grow or improve physically and mentally.

A great deal of time will be spent this year communicating and writing about issues that concern both you and your community/interest groups. You may join together with others in order to achieve a common goal. If you are already involved in a cause or are an activist or lobbyist, this is a very powerful year for making a stand and achieving both recognition and publicity for your endeavors.

In 2015, you will be rather pugnacious with your words, both written and spoken – you will convey your ideas with more aggression and passion. You may try to stir up opinion by being somewhat controversial. It is a year when you will be inclined to say what you think and not to hold back. It is not a case of blurting things out, but rather that you are making a calculated attempt to sway opinion and get your ideas out there.

For journalists (many Gemini are in this field as they are well suited to it), writers, political activists, academics, researchers, inventors and educators this will be an inspiring year when you can make breakthroughs on many levels. Your mental approach is fresh and fearless; you are not bound by convention, you have the courage of your convictions and the energy to push ideas forward and convey them to others.

If within your line of work you need to be able to think quickly, debate and come up with facts and figures on the spot, then you are going to have much success this year. Mentally, you are sharp and have an abundance of energy: a great time to make a good impression and certainly a productive time for communications and marketing.

Self-confidence and assertiveness are not usually the Gemini strongpoint, but as the year goes on you will find that you begin to find your feet and will fare very well where confrontation and strong will is called for. Gemini are a very positive sign, but Geminis tend to be passive and to adapt rather than creating and influencing; however, this year you will find that you are more inclined to take that first step and to be the one that initiates. You will use your ability with words and your talent with people to open doors for yourself and find quick solutions to problems.

It's a very busy year, and you will have to be versatile, which to be fair is a Gemini strength. You must be able to multitask, and your work routine will have to have flexibility built in. If you have a routine or a set 9-5 style daily plan, this may get shaken up this year. Life and work will call for you to play many different roles and to quickly become an expert in some new fields. You will have to think on your feet and may have to make some very quick decisions, which could quite dramatically change your lifestyle.

A sudden promotion or job relocation could throw your life into chaos for a short period, and you will have to accept that the new opportunities although exciting can create dilemmas. You may feel under pressure for much of the year as so much is expected of you, and you will have much to learn. A new job, career or home could mean new skills or even languages to learn. This is, however, a year when you are very much in control – even if it does not feel like it at the time, you are indeed in control, and you can influence events and outcomes.

Gemini like to avoid conflict and will often opt for the fence-sitting position; however, events this year will force you to nail your colors to the mast and either pick sides or get stuck in. Do not shy away if your leadership is called on in a tense, emotionally charged conflict as you can use your people skills to resolve issues and bring situations to a positive conclusion – use you power wisely and with confidence.

2015 is a year of interesting opportunities and exciting changes – however, many of these changes will require hard work to either adjust or to make things function. While some things will fall into place very easily, others will not, and this should not demoralize you and make you doubt yourself. It is just an indication that nothing should be taken for granted and that nothing can replace a good strategy and groundwork.

For Gemini who have felt a little bored or in a rut, 2015 is the perfect time to make that change you have wanted: go for that new job, move to that new city, take a course, get dating again or ditch the troubled relationship. Like in the previous paragraph, change is due for you now, and some obstacles should not put you off – make changes and work through the problems systematically. The long-term changes that happen now are positive; the stresses and resulting problems are temporary.

Mental health comes into focus in 2015, and it is time to take a look at issues like stress, depression, anxiety, phobias and addictions – we all have these to some degree. This year, you must recognize and own up to any issues you have that may be limiting your enjoyment or productivity in life and recognize these and find ways of addressing or solving them.

Relationships can be tricky this year as you are giving out mixed signals – on one hand, you look really confident and are behaving rather assertively and even more aggressively in arguments. You seem tougher and more determined; however, your more forceful attitude in 2015 belies the fact that you need emotional support. You are certainly capable of providing firm friendship and love to those who need your support, and you will cheer them on; however, you may not feel as if you are getting the emotional affirmation you need in return. It may be hard for you to show your vulnerable side, and there is a strong urge to put on a brave face and soldier on. You need to show more emotion and be more open about your emotions to get the support you need. However, this year, your emotions and feelings run very deep and are not easy to explain. Even if you are getting support from friends and loved ones, it may not fill the gap or be enough solace for you.

There is a searching quality to your emotional and spiritual life right now, which has somewhat disconcerted you and thrown you off balance. Gemini is a very rational and logical sign, and when the emotions you are having are impossible to explain away or understand, you tend to feel off center and confused. Gemini who are in strong relationships or who have firm family support will get closer and closer to that person or that family member right now as they will understand you without you saying a word. It is a time when your closest bonds with people are reaffirmed and when those that really know and care about you can help.

You are less interested in casual relationships this year and much more focused on nurturing existing relationships or pursuing relationships that you see as having potential. In love, you are quite demanding of affection to make you feel secure, and if you do not get that you may become possessive and a little jealous. Careful you do not alienate your loved ones with criticism no matter how well-intentioned. You must be careful not to become too emotionally dependent on others this year.

We all have different categories of friends, and they can fulfil our needs in differing ways; this year it will be the deeper friendships and the people with whom you can share your most private thoughts and emotions that will be of most importance. You may also be able to help those you care for as you have a deeper insight into people and their hidden personalities this year.

Rest is essential this year, and you must get enough sleep and eat proteins and Vitamin B complex which support your nervous system and brain function. If you can meditate or find a mental cut off method, this will really be of assistance. It is a very taxing and busy year, and you will have to put in constant mental effort, which is why rest and mental breathers are so essential. Look after your chest, and if you smoke, it's really time to give it up this year. Chest infections are common with the transits to your Mercury and so take extra precautions and eat plenty of fresh food.

You may find yourself being more defensive and suspicious this year – your perspectives on things around you are changing, and you are not sure who you can trust and rely on. As the year goes on, it will become clear who your true allies are. Sometimes you may simply be feeling suspicious due to stress, and it may be nothing – do not over-estimate these feelings until you have more substantial evidence.

You are both optimistic and perceptive this year, and so it is a key time to evaluate your life and look forward – you are very open to new possibilities and to avenues that you have not thought about before. You can see your life with a new maturity and a better grasp of your deeper needs; thus it is a great time to plan. You are also very focused and realistic, and so what better combination for creating a new life strategy – optimism with realism.

You are very creative and inspired this year and so for any artistic pursuits you can be very productive.

You may pursue an interest in spirituality or the occult this year, either for guidance or as a form of searching and self-discovery. This may lead to the discovery of a latent talent.

It is essential this year to own your emotions – be honest about them: let the positive ones out without holding back and deal with the negative ones with more openness. Suppressed emotions or ones you are not acknowledging may have a detrimental effect on the way you communicate and relate to others.

A large degree of insight and understanding can help you to communicate on a very different level with great effectiveness: you are able to tap into a mood or trend and use that constructively within your business, artistic pursuits or in relationships. Do not use this in a selfish way. Your gift this year is to be able to connect with people you do not normally get on with; you are in a very different space mentally, and this can allow you to empathize and have more productive relationships with these people.

A year of motivation and mental determination. There is no doubt you can achieve goals and open doors for yourself. You must allow yourself to let go in relationships to achieve the full level of emotional connectivity and warmth you desire. It will be a very enlightening year, when you will seek something to fulfil you on an ethereal level. Use the foresight and initiative you have this year to plan positively for the future.

LIFE

A very hectic and even chaotic start to the New Year. Your first priority is to get your finances in order, or you could be in for a nasty surprise mid-month. Do not put anything off, and make sure that anything contractual is tied up before the 22nd of Jan when Mercury turns retrograde. This is not a month to mix friendship with money: do not borrow or lend to a friend as it will become very complicated and create stressful bother.

You may find that your friendship circle and the events that are part of that i.e. weddings, christenings, baby showers, parties, etc. are beyond your budget this month, and that may cause you a dilemma – remember that sometimes a small, personalized gift that did not cost much means more that some standardized item, even if it was expensive.

In January, you are feeling highly restless and you are looking to squeeze out of commitments that you feel take too much of your time and effort, and which give little back; you may have been roped into PTAs, a focus group, a treasurer position or something of that nature. You are now ready to throw the towel in, and it is not about being a quitter, it is about streamlining your life and your routine and getting out of what is not essential.

QVC is the motto as you start this New Year, and I am not talking about the shopping channel – everything in your life must pass the QVC test, i.e. Quality, Value added and Contentment. Make quality use of your time, be sure what you do adds value to your life and creates contentment. If activities this month are stressful and confusing, drop them, don't go there, it isn't worth it.

Watch your diet carefully – this is a month to detox.

LOVE

Relations with you and your partner should be harmonious this month, and you will crack on with plenty of activities together – it is a month of doing things and achieving things as a team. You will feel quite happy for him/her to take the lead.

It is really important to work at relationships now – do not expect quick fixes or easy solutions to the problems you may face. The issues are not as great as you think they are, and this month when things are rather harmonious, work at all the things you enjoy and do well together, instead of obsessing about what isn't right.

I really do not advise trying to have in-depth discussions about your sex life or deeper relationship issues this month as you will not have the patience to really listen, and you may jump to the wrong conclusion. Concentrate on having fun and getting out of yourselves – break the rut and learn to have fun together again.

New relationships may struggle this month and arguments over money could push you both to breaking point. As Geminis are rather impulsive this month, new relationships could well spark up, but they are unlikely to last as you are not in tune with your real needs right now.

CAREER

Office politics can frustrate your plans at work. You are keen to create change and innovate both with communications and the PR side of your business. You are full of ideas right now and rather keen to provide leadership on a number of issues. However, you may experience opposition from other staff members or colleagues who are resistant to change or who see your enthusiasm as a threat.

It could well be that you are new to a role or job, and you are not quite au fait with the vested interests and sensitivities of the people you work with. Play your cards closer to your chest when dealing with people at work as some are not being very upfront with you.

Some of the plans you have for your business or your ambitions at work may be delayed by you having to acquire new skills or pass some sort of test. You can quickly master the required skills once you put your mind to it.

Do not neglect legal issues within all your communications. When it comes to clients and money received or paid, be meticulous about your records.

Money spent this month within your business should be towards training and investing in staff, rather than capital expenditure.

LIFE

A highly sociable and enjoyable month. You are amicable and passionate about what you do. A very good time to initiate creative projects or even plan a party or social event. You may be involved in planning an event at work, which will help with team building and morale.

You are the go-to person this month when it comes to resolving differences – you can be highly persuasive and to bring people together in a spirit of reconciliation.

A month for pursuing and also rediscovering your creative hobbies – you are very creative and energetic right now and need an outlet for this energy.

Take the bull by the horns and use this time for creating beauty and harmony in your world – whether this means a good clear-out before redecorating or smoothing over relations with family members, you do not usually see eye to eye with. Harmony and fun are what matters right now, and your joie de vivre and spontaneity will make you a pleasure to be around.

It is a very impulsive month – maybe it's better to stay away from temptation as you may spend first and think later.

LOVE

A fabulous month for romance – Valentine's Day will be full of sparkle.

New relationships are bound to start up as you are highly attractive and are giving off a fun-loving vibe. You may hook up with a family friend or someone you bump into from your past, and love may blossom.

Full of emotional warmth and sexual energy, your relationships will not only be running smoothly but will contain more passion and zest than usual. You will be the initiator in both new and old relationships. You are very sensual right now, and the physicality of the relationship is vital; you will be rather demanding, but the signs are that your advances will be well received.

I think there will be much romance this month: movies, nights at the ballet/opera, visits to local beauty spots and lovely meals out.

CAREER

A very prosperous time if you work in the hospitality industry or in the creative arts. This is a fortunate time to expand your client base or sell more products with a new sales initiative. Improving communication with your customers, giving loyalty discounts, free samples, competitions or themes days are key ways to create more interest and enthusiasm for your products.

There may be some setback businesswise this month in terms of long-term goals and plans. It's a case of back to the drawing board. Issues to do with financing and insuring projects may be the problem, or it could be getting more cash injected into your department. Plans are on ice until you can restructure some of the details. Your judgment on matters of financial importance is key, and many of your decisions will come under scrutiny later on, and so take your time and be sure.

Diligent preparation with some bold decisions is what is called for; you will not be afraid to stick your neck out, but do be prepared to answer for it and defend your actions. You may not always be in the right place at the right time this month, but do not let that frustrate you, just keep working around the problems and improvising.

LIFE

There is a great emphasis on reputation and status in life this month. You may well find yourself rewarded, especially if you are in a field like research, academia or teaching. Whatever your career, or even if you are not currently working, you will think about your status in life and how you want to be seen by others.

If your public profile is important to you, this is a terrific month to re-launch or rebrand yourself – find a new audience or expand beyond your current genre.

You may find yourself thrust into a new role within your community where you can be instrumental in changing the lives of others – this may be a charity or voluntary role. Using your talents for the common goal without expecting a payback can be the key to changing your life direction in a positive way for months to come.

This month will see a burst of energy and you should use that to make new beginnings, and it does not matter how small or in what area of life they are – anything new which you begin now can have a greater impact on your confidence, well-being and life prospects than you think.

Your children will need you more than usual this month, and you may feel torn between the urge to advise and the urge to control and protect. You simply have to let them make their own mistakes sometimes.

Creative projects can be hugely emotionally fulfilling this month.

LOVE

You may want to take a few small risks in love this March – now what you regard as 'risk' really depends on your personality, but a risk could be anything from trying a new way to meet a partner, breaking a rule you have set for yourself, i.e. no workplace romances, asking someone you hardly know out, etc. If you are already in a relationship, a risk may mean suggesting a new sexual toy or activity. It could even mean talking about a sexual problem you have not had the ability to talk about before. Take the bull by the horns, and you may surprise yourself. Not taking risks means getting into ruts, which can be both boring and self-defeating – break the mold this month and do something romantically or sexually that you would not usually do.

In relationships, this may be the time you begin to talk about having a baby or adding to the family.

Love can easily blossom this spring, so don't let anything hold you back.

CAREER

There is a slight conflict between work and home this month, and events and commitments at home may interfere with your work routine or your ability to concentrate on your work. Your clients or your boss will be understanding as long as you explain things and give everyone enough time.

For those of you who work with children, in psychology or in caring for others in some way, this will be a month where you experience great reward and satisfaction from your work. You may find you gain an insight into your own nature or deeper needs from those you are helping. The people you help or council may actually end up helping you in a karmic way.

Principles and family values are at the heart of business this month, and so make sure that if you are the employer you are fair and inclusive about the way you employ mothers with young children or in providing flexible working hours for your staff who have family commitments.

I spoke about reputation and status – this month you want your business to have a reputation for being family-friendly and having strong principles.

If you are an employee, make sure that every decision you take this month is a principled and fair one. Stand up for yourself if you feel your values are not appreciated or considered in the workplace.

APRIL

LIFE

You are courageous and decisive this month. You will be called upon to provide moral leadership on issues at home, work and within your social life. You will have a surplus of energy and will be able to work for long periods without becoming tired and drained.

You are the Alpha Male/Female this month, even if that is not a role you usually take on. You can be successful in leadership roles as you are encouraging more than bossy, and that wins you respect.

You are likely to take up sporting pursuits this month, but more for the enjoyment than the competitive aspect – you are enthusiastic, not fiercely competitive right now.

This is rather a lucky month, when things will tend to flow and where you can be more productive than usual. Even the humdrum routines will be easier to bear. As you are feeling confident this month, use the time to tackle anything you would usually shy away from. Take some chances in terms of applying for new jobs or new positions, entering a competition, etc. I am not suggesting you initiate major changes right now, but this is a great time to test the water with a nothing ventured, nothing gained attitude.

LOVE

Give and take is the theme in relationships. Your partner may accuse you of being selfish and demanding, which is not really fair; you are both just not on the same page this month. Sometimes our loved ones want tangible evidence of our commitment, and that is the case this month; you really need to put in extra effort to show him/her that you care. This means listening more, helping out, taking an interest, going the extra mile.

Often we do not realize how we take those we love for granted, and so it is not a bad thing to reaffirm that commitment and love by making some extra effort.

It is possible that you may have some arguments at the start of the month – try and hold your tongue as you are likely to regret saying things later on. Do not jump to conclusions and try and be as fair-minded as possible, even in heated debates. Arguing and getting angry will not really get either of you anywhere, especially as you will tend to get stubborn and more entrenched in your views. Drop the arguing about small issues and think about ways to constructively balance your needs. This is not a month where an argument clears the air, it's a month where you need to keep trying and keep remembering what each of you said in the argument in terms of what you need and expect from each other.

CAREER

Cooperation is key this month – even if you have to put differences aside to cooperate with a competitor or a colleague you really cannot stand. Be diplomatic and do not be intimidated. Teamwork and compromise may be very much a part of what you have to do work-wise this month.

You are full of strength and courage right now and should not shy away from any challenge at work as you can do it. Be positive as this is a really fortunate month when things should fall into place.

In business, issues wider than your usual frame of reference will have to be taken into account, and you may need to seek legal advice or even hire a translator.

Be fair in everything you do, and you will be beyond reproach. If you encourage others to be fair and committed to the end result, things can be very productive despite differences.

LIFE

Your responses are lightning quick this month – you can react fast to new information, you can pick up new skills, and you are highly observant. You are also highly strung and may jump to conclusions at times or react in a snappy, irritable manner.

You really want to get things done, and patience is not your strong point. Being in a rush and doing chores slapdash can be your downfall, and you should not sacrifice accuracy for speed, no matter how boring or unimportant something feels.

You have quite a short attention span this month and cannot concentrate for long – if you can plan your month, try and arrange your schedule so that projects, study or chores which are laborious and need long hours of concentration are completed before or after May. For May, plan a variety of things that take advantage of your energy and your ability to rush about and get things done fast.

LOVE

If your partner is not feeling as energetic as you, you may need to spend time apart this month. Geminis are restless and need to burn off excess energy. You are finding it hard to sit still and relax, and you need to be busy or entertained constantly. If your partner is also a mutable sign, this could be an exciting month where you try new things, travel and socialize together.

You are in a jocular mood and ready for friendly debate – be sure that others do not take you too seriously and take offence. You can be quick to talk and might be prone to talking out of turn or gossiping – do be careful that what you say does not come back to hurt you or someone you love. This is a month to be very clear in all communications, say what you have to say to someone's face, rather than letting it go around the houses getting distorted. Someone may twist your words to cause trouble within your love life. Be very wary of what you say to extended family members; in fact, it is better to keep anything you have to say about your private or romantic life to yourself.

A good time to start new relationships; however, the fizz may soon be gone, but that does not mean that a fast and furious love affair cannot be fulfilling.

CAREER

A great month for market research, starting a new course, learning a new skill or connecting with new clients. Novelty is the theme. Look to incorporate new IT systems and more effective methods of office management to streamline your day and save time.

Look after your social media platforms, i.e. Facebook, g+ or LinkedIn and make sure that they are updated – many opportunities to be headhunted or gain clients are to be had online, so make sure you manage your own and your company's online image.

You will definitely want to ensure important contracts and deals are closed before May 19, when Mercury turns retrograde. Make sure that all the i's are dotted etc. and since you are not in the best frame of mind for spotting detail, make sure a colleague or family member reads through anything you are putting forward, be it a report, paper, contract, quote, etc.

You are highly curious this month, and so it is a great time to be reading reports, reading the newspaper and keeping up with trends and current affairs, which could give you a competitive advantage.

A busy month for travelling locally for business and corresponding. If you deal in trade, business will be very busy indeed.

LIFE

You may begin this month feeling a little daunted by what you need to do; you have set yourself a very high bar this year and need to keep up with the standard and pace you have set. Even though you are seeing concrete results, some aspects of your life may need to go into reverse for a short time while you check your spiritual sat nav and continue the journey in a slightly different direction.

Not a good month to make decisions about your life and overall life direction; you are just not thinking clearly enough, and there are too many confusing factors which could lead to a skewed perspective.

Buying and selling both in your business or personal life are not favored. Worry and anxiety can plague you at this time and so avoid alcohol, stimulants or anything that can exacerbate these issues. A lot of the things troubling you seem worse than they are. Get enough sleep, exercise and fresh food and top up your vitamins and proteins with a healthy shake.

Your spiritual life matters to you right now, and you will devote time to activities that you feel help you to get in touch with your higher self. If you do visit a psychic or clairvoyant this month, be skeptical as you are highly impressionable, and it is best that you sit on their advice for a while before acting on it.

LOVE

It will become clear this month if the relationship you are in has long-term potential, and you will not shy aware from frank heart-to-hearts in order to establish whether there really is communication at a deeper level or if it is just a superficial passing attraction.

Long-term stable relationships may suffer from a breakdown in communication for the following reasons. For one, you are highly sensitive right now and may read too much into something that is not very important. Secondly, you are very idealistic, and even perfect behavior on the part of your spouse would still fall short of the mark somewhere. Thirdly, when you are speaking and conveying your thoughts and emotions, you are not really listening to the reply. Communication has to be two way and right now, it's all coming from you, and you are assuming what is coming back rather than listening to what is actually being said.

CAREER

Resistance from colleagues and superiors can be frustrating, and you will have to be at your most mentally agile and quick-witted to persuade them of your argument. Frustrations in terms of bureaucracy, red tape, procedure or dealing with government departments can make your job tricky and cause quite a bit of extra paperwork and hassle.

Changes in the law may also affect your daily routine and how you work, and this will take a while to get used to. Diligence and persistence are the keys to success this month, so keep your fine tooth comb at the ready.

This can be misconstrued as a negative time, when in fact it is actually a time of concrete challenge, appraisal and re-planning or re-positioning due to outside factors. Any loose ends or unclear fussy thinking will get flagged up, and you will have to tighten up and outline your thoughts and strategy more clearly.

Do not think you can pull the wool over your boss's eyes this month – mistakes, oversights or deceptions will come to light.

Trust your gut instincts about people.

Artistically, this is a brilliantly creative month.

LIFE

Family relationships, especially those with women are in focus this month. Tolerance and acceptance are the key issues in getting over hurdles in understanding. Bridges must be re-built, and family ties reestablished this month.

Your nurturing and loving side is at the forefront as you display emotions and affection. Family matters this month, and spending quality time with your parents and your children is fulfilling and emotionally nourishing. Your extended family may come together to celebrate or to support a family member who needs some help.

Motherhood is especially fulfilling and rewarding right now, and you can really appreciate the bond you have with your children. If you do not have children, you may feel very broody and begin to think in that direction.

Eating and catering are very much part of the month as they usually are when family come together; you may be involved in making many of the plans regarding purchasing and organizing of the food. Events will center on your home.

It is very much a back to your roots month with renewed appreciation of who you are and where you come from. You may get out old photos and albums as your children start to take an interest in how you grew up. You may feel inspired to write about something which happened in your past and which shaped you.

LOVE

Your understanding and caring nature will go a long way to ensuring that love relationships are close, warm and happy. You are in a very giving, inclusive and gentle mood and are craving closeness. You will demand attention from your partner, and you need to feel that warmth back right now; if your partner is distant, stressed or emotionally unresponsive you can be very moody and sulky.

You are putting a lot of effort in this month in terms of relationships, and if you do not see an equally loving response, your feelings will be hurt. My advice is to not put it all out there; be loving by all means, but as soon as you feel it is not being reciprocated, pull back and protect yourself. Do not keep giving to someone who is not in the mood or the right frame of mind to give back.

In new relationships, the impulse is to be very open and full-on emotionally – this can set you up for a disappointment, especially as since you are rather sensitive right now, you may even take a small insignificant rebuff to heart.

When your partner responds, this can be an amazing month for love, warmth and really meaningful sex.

CAREER

If you are not employed or are looking to change your employment, this month is an ideal one to examine the options closely to work from home or even work more hours from home. Think about how you could increase time spent with family and your own flexibility if you spent more hours working from home and less travelling into work. Talk to people online who are already doing this via forums, g+, etc. and see if you can get any tips or advice.

Gemini who write for a living will find this an extremely fruitful month when they will be inspired, especially when writing on romantic and emotional issues as well as those to do with nature, animals and healthy lifestyles.

Geminis, who are in teaching, may find that their pupils come to them for advice and guidance.

In all aspects of business, this is a time to invest and save money. In terms of investments, look towards traditional and evergreen stocks rather than start-ups or teckie firms.

In any job or business, do not allow sentimentality over some aspect of your business to cloud your judgment. Sometimes you have to let something go for the better.

LIFE

This can be a stop-start month with you wanting to put your foot on the gas, but having to slam on the brake every five minutes due to something happening.

You must look deeper and ask yourself: is it really the outside world stopping me in my tracks, or is it a nagging lack of confidence within me that is being projected onto the outside world and causing these obstacles? Have a deep think about what you are doing: do you really want to choose this direction? Are you 100% behind it? Are you indeed conflicted? Are the obstacles to do with your partner or your home life? When you have the answers to these questions you can detect the core root of the obstacles, and you may find that you can either go forward without hitches or realize that you were barking up the wrong tree, anyway.

There may be difficulties keeping everyone happy this month as you are pulled between commitments and obligations to people. Each commitment is just as important, and you cannot be all things to all people no matter how much you want to. You will end up having to choose and having to disappoint someone, but as long as you make the decision in plenty of time instead of delaying until the last minute, you can still end up saving the day.

LOVE

Single Gemini may well meet someone quite accidentally during either study, travel or a legal matter to whom they are immediately drawn. This person may either be older or mature for their age, and the relationship can get off the ground rather fast.

This month is a positive one for Geminis, who are themselves older or divorced to find love. A great maturity in the way you approach and handle relationships is an asset right now. A relationship that begins now can be rather surprising and can really widen your horizons.

In ongoing relationships it is important to uphold your responsibilities, there may be times this month where you feel restless and are wondering if the grass is not greener. You should not let any feelings of wanderlust jeopardize your relationships: be responsible and recognize that any relationship needs reliability and hard work, there is no such thing as greener grass or a free lunch either, OK!

Work that you put into relationships, even when it's tough and not that exciting, will be rewarded.

CAREER

This is an ideal month for business organization, formatting contracts and dealing with legal issues. You must seek to work with others within your field – a collaboration with another expert can help solidify your reputation. You may look to join up with other businesses in a joint marketing campaign or perhaps host a competition with other similar businesses. Look to see what you have in common with other businesses, i.e. product, location, similar customers and see how you can combine resources to improve trade for you all. Get in touch with the local chamber of commerce for support.

Take responsibilities towards your coworkers and seniors seriously, do not try and show anyone up or pull rank as it will not go down well this month. Make sure your company and those you work with are socially responsible in terms of being as 'green' or as environmental as possible and with regards to workers' rights.

This can be a very fortunate month in terms of promotion for those who work in the police, law enforcement, and departments of state and local authorities.

LIFE

Your mind is sharp, and you are keenly perceptive this month. You can get to the heart of the matter, and this can be ideal if you need to edit or redraft work or if you have to use your words very succinctly to have a big impact.

The aspects this month favour mass communications, and so if you need to publish something or get your voice heard, on a matter of importance to you personally or to your work, this is an ideal time. Your words and the way in which you speak and communicate will have a very big impact and lasting effect.

Choose your words carefully as what you say can have a more dramatic effect than you think. Play your cards close to your chest and do not be as trusting as you usually would with colleagues and extended family members. If you have a secret, then do not tell anybody if you want it to stay a secret.

You can be highly persuasive during this period, and so if you have to manipulate a situation to your advantage, this is an opportune time. You are very strong-minded right now, and you are far more likely to sway opinion than to change your own opinions.

LOVE

"We can't go on together with suspicious minds."

The Elvis classic may be apt this month as you are prone to distrust and perhaps are reading too much into your partner's actions. You are craving attention, love, and affection right now, and you must be aware of a certain Diva-like behavior which may have the effect of alienating rather than bringing you closer to your partner. When you do not get what you want when you want it from your lover, you may become paranoid about his/her feelings about you, instead of realizing that perhaps your demands for attention are quite exhausting right now.

If you feel a little neglected, do not resort to cell phone checking and controlling behavior, just go off on your own and enjoy yourself. This month should be about you feeling good and having fun; do not look for all your love and attention from your partner and then sulk if you don't get it. If your partner is up for it, great; however, if he/she isn't then do not sit at home, get amongst your friends and live it up socially.

For single Gemini, this is a highly enjoyable month socially, but the need to interrogate potential new partners and get intimate (both physically and emotionally) quickly may play against you, so take more time romantically.

CAREER

An excellent month for due diligence and fine-tuning of strategies and reports.

As I mentioned before, this is an outstanding period for Geminis who write speeches, edit publications, write investigative journalism or do research as your ability to sort the wheat from the chaff and then communicate what you find in an insightful, impactful way is excellent.

Timing is also very important in your career – do not expect everything to be linear. Your strategy should be to push forward, then pause, re-evaluate, alter course slightly and push forward again. Be very alert to what is going on with colleagues and competitors, and do not play your hand too soon, be a dark horse and do not act in isolation – keep watching what others are doing and learning from their mistakes.

Geminis are indeed always clever with words, but in September this ability is even more pronounced and can be used very effectively in sales, negotiations and getting to the bottom of complicated matters.

LIFE

It is essential right now to turn the volume from the outside world down and tune inwards and listen to your inner voice. It is also time to give others a voice as people will come to you as they sense that you are receptive to their emotions and able to understand their dilemmas.

This is a time of heightened empathy; however, you must not be an emotional sponge that soaks up the problems of others and takes them onto yourself. Yes, you can be helpful and supportive to others and use your level of deeper understanding to help them, but boundaries are vital.

Listen to the messages your body is giving you. Health issues right now should be taken as a clear message to cut back, detox, get more rest or eat more of the right food. You have probably been eating a lot worse than you think lately, and your body is saying STOP. Get more water, fresh air, and light exercise. You may begin to look into new diets, i.e. Paleo, Ketogenic, gluten-free, Mediterranean, etc. not only as a way of losing weight, but as a way of increasing your energy. This is a period where you can turn your health around by starting a new regime of healthy eating – so check out what's new in the world of eating. There are 100s of great quality Kindle books on various diets with delicious recipes and motivational stories to help you with common digestive, allergic and health problems.

Dreams are very important this month; they are your connection to the subconscious, and you should listen to what the subconscious is saying.

LOVE

Again, boundaries are really important this October in your close relationships. No matter how close you are, there have to be some aspects of your personality or your personal space which are off limits. Now your partner may already know what you don't like, but have you ever noticed how people encroach more and more until they need a refresher course? You may have to have a firm and diplomatic discussion about what you are not happy or comfortable with, just to set that boundary back in place.

All relationships have secrets, and you should not feel guilty about having them; they add mystery and the sense that there is more to discover about you. You need to let your partner know this month that although you have secrets, he/she has nothing to worry about.

Everything I say above should be easy as communication in relationships is excellent this month, and so what better time to have a sincere discussion about emotional and sexual issues? You are far more likely to feel able to have a frank and loving discussion than an argument.

Sexual energy is high, and your enthusiasm and positive attitude will ensure that your relationships are warm and loving.

New relationships can get off the ground very quickly this month, but do remember those boundaries.

CAREER

A strong month for PR, promotional and sales initiatives. Yes, Christmas is coming, and that means the busiest time of year for sales. Gemini should do especially well this month in sales of consumer goods, beauty products, leisure goods and luxury goods.

Versatility is the key this month with you involved in a variety of different jobs and roles; you will have to be a jack of all trades. At times, you may feel overwhelmed with all the details, but you will find the challenge and variety stimulating. Travel both local and national is a possibility.

You may be dealing with the press, i.e. sending out press releases, doing promotional interviews, etc. This is an ideal time to launch a new product, new book, etc.

For Gemini, who are unemployed, take the bull by the horns and take on a job even if it is a seasonal, short-term contract as there are opportunities now that if taken can grow into something more.

LIFE

You will have to be quite strict with yourself this month as discipline is required; it's almost like a self-imposed austerity where you are looking to achieve targets, i.e. weight loss for a Christmas Party or saving money to spend in December. You have the willpower, and you can achieve anything you set your mind to.

You can be rather uptight this month, and you will react strongly to criticism, especially if you think that it is unfair – defend yourself by all means, but pick your battles wisely as not everything is important enough to lose sleep over.

You could be instrumental in aiding someone who is going through a problem or crisis similar to something you went through in the past – you will have both practical and spiritual advice, which can be of great assistance. In a similar vein, you will often play the role of wise friend or mentor this month.

LOVE

Gemini in new relationships should avoid showing vulnerability and speaking about previous relationships. New relationships should not be approached from a standpoint of neediness or over-eagerness – play it cool and do not limit your options. Single Gemini have the tendency to pin their hopes on someone too quickly, instead of staying available and playing the field a bit.

Buried hurts and angers may resurface in relationships – use this as an opportunity to get to the bottom of the problem and draw a line under it. Your ego and pride can actually be the biggest obstacle to getting closer in relationships – try to set ego and pride issues aside when you have deep conversations; otherwise, it can take time to resolve things. Be sure not to project issues from precious relationships onto the current one – do not assume that since an ex did XYZ, your current partner is likely to do the same; you are, in fact, tarring all relationships with the negativity of one of your past experiences.

In some cases, pride and a certain arrogance can be an overcompensation for feelings of self- doubt and lack of self-worth – think more about how your confidence or lack of it can be impacting on your relationships.

CAREER

This is a very important time as you will have to make moral judgments and difficult decisions. While decisions you make will make total sense from a logical and practical perspective, they may be hard for you to live with morally, but you have to do what you have to do. Some of these decisions may cast a cloud over you for part of this month, and you may feel like Atlas with the weight of the world on your shoulders. You can be assured, however, that you will act in a just and fair way, and you must be decisive and clear.

While this is a prosperous time for you in business, it is also very demanding mentally, and this month will see you having to put in a sustained effort – not a time to take your foot off the gas.

Keep an eye on financial figures, data and statistics that relate to your industry or business this month as what looks great on the surface may not be so good comparatively and vice versa. You need a firm grasp of financial facts to make good decisions and so do not gloss over these and make assumptions.

LIFE

Feeling original, full of fizz and full of life, what a terrific way to end the year. Your strong willpower, creative ability, and motivation to get things done fast will see a very productive end to 2015.

In fact, December will be very busy, you will have lots on the go and quite a few exciting last minute events to attend. Feeling in the mood for novelty, you may be the force behind your family doing something totally different or unconventional this festive season.

You have a feeling of freedom and confidence about you as if you have finally shaken off the lingering doubts that came and went this year. You are rather a party animal, and no party will be complete without you – you may take center stage at events with your stories and humor.

There is a big focus on extended family, and you will make an effort to be as inclusive as possible when planning get-togethers; you do not want anyone to feel left out or to miss out on the fun. You may go the extra mile for an older relative or to support a family member or friend who is alone over the holidays. Being surrounded by family is what you really need on an emotional level, and the positive vibes of the holidays will set you up in a confident and pro-active mood for 2016.

2015 ends with a celebration of what you have achieved all year; you are taking a large dose of strength, belief and energy into 2016, which you are excited about already. It may be that you have some exciting plans for 2016, you are very charged up and feeling rejuvenated and ready to tackle anything. The start of 2016 will be inspiring and exciting as you are alert to possibilities and have the willpower to make anything happen.

LOVE

Your partner will appreciate the fact that you are devoting just as much time to his/her family as you are to yours this Christmas – whose family to spend the holidays with is often a bone of contention. However, you are going out of your way to be fair and accommodating. You are very perceptive and rather inventive right now, and so you tend to know how to please and who needs what.

If you have been with someone for many years but have never been married, you may rush off to the registry office for a gunshot wedding. Yes, you are impulsive right now, and that can certainly extend to relationships: a sudden decision to tie the knot or a new relationship that becomes serious quickly. You have a desire right now to cement things within your love life; there is a strong sense of settling down. This said you may decide to move in with a current boyfriend next year or even buy a house together. Whatever stage of a relationship you are at, you are ready to take it to the next level of commitment.

Sex is earthy, sensual and very passionate. The more committed you feel your partner is, the better the sex is. Casual sexual relations are not as relaxing or satisfying this month; it is sex within stable, secure relationships that really rings all the right bells.

Sex can be quite racy and quirky, so make sure you visit the lingerie shop for yourself or to buy your gal a pressie.

CAREER

For those of you involved in creative careers, you are filled with ideas and motivation for next year; you may spend quite a bit of time over December researching and planning for next year's project. You have a vision of where you want to be, and you are very inspired by the opportunities you see. You are feeling very competitive and have a burning desire to outpace and outsmart your competitors in 2016. Geminis are not always driven to win, you guys like to take part and get the most of things; however, the urge to win is strong now. You feel you have reached a stage where you have worked hard and now have an edge that you can take forward. You must pick your confidantes and co-workers with care – you need people around that truly support you and do not detract from what you are doing.

You are feeling that your work is fulfilling on a spiritual and emotional level right now, and that is what is propelling you forward with such gusto.

Geminis, who do not feel like their work satisfies their higher needs will have that same drive to find a new career or job.

December is an excellent time for Geminis, who work in IT, science, technology and emerging industries.

THANK YOU SO MUCH for BUYING and READING GEMINI 2015

If you enjoyed it, please leave a review by clicking here

CPSIA information can be obtained at www.ICGtesting.com
Printed in the USA
LVOW11s1450120115

422492LV00002B/333/P